How You Too Can Be

Successful and Make

Lots of Money Even If

You Have No Talent

By

Ernie Braveboy

Get Your Free Copy of

How to be a Real Estate Millionaire

To Get Your Free Copy, Open the Link

https://ebraveboy_3ee2.gr8.com/

Introduction

I want to thank you and congratulate you for buying the book, *"How You Too Can Be Successful and Make Lots of Money Even If You Have No Talent"*.

This book has actionable information on how you can succeed in life and make tons of money even if you have no talent.

Most self-help book, especially those on the subject of how to achieve success, preach the same hokum:

"To achieve success, you have to follow your passion and capitalize on your talents or strengths."

From a general perspective, this is good advice.

If you are pursuing something you are naturally good at, which is what talent is: *an innate gift,* you will achieve success that much faster because you will have the innate motivation and drive to excel at that thing as well as the determination to persevere (be gritty) when tough times come calling, which they will.

Take the example of Sir Mohamed Muktar Jama "Mo" Farah, Britain's most successful distance runner. There is no doubt in anyone's mind that Mo Farah is a "talented" athlete. The kind of success he has achieved can only come from someone who has attuned his talents to life's pursuits.

Here is the thing though; do you think talent is all it took for Farah to win the many Olympic Gold medals he has won in the men's 5000 meters and 10,000 meters, 1500 meters, and even marathons? Is talent all it took for him to become the successful person he is today? The answer is NO!

While Farah's innate talent is indeed running, to become the great athlete the world knows of today, he had to put in tons of hours into mastering his craft. He had to learn many things such as dieting, how his foot contacts the ground using the mid-foot strike, strength training, and many other things.

He also had to make many sacrifices (he trains twice a day, goes to high altitude camps, trains his muscles, etc.). He had to do all this long before he achieved the success he has today and it is because of doing all this that he achieved the success he enjoys today.

What does this tell you about success? Take a wild guess and then compare it to the following statement:

Mo's story (and the stories of many other successful people) implies that even when talent is innate, excellence is not. To excel, even in something you are talented in, you have to practice: you have to dedicate time to that pursuit. Therefore, talent does not equal success. Success equals deliberate and consistent practice.

Will Durant once said, *"We are what we repeatedly do. Excellence, then, is not an act, but a habit."* No words ring truer. To achieve success, any type of success, you do not need a natural affinity to that thing, no! All you need is to do that thing consistently until you master it and achieve excellence.

"Do something that complements your talent" is great advice.

In an instance where you intimately know your talents (your strong suits), you should pursue such a career or life path because when you are naturally good at what you do, your work and play symbiosis will be great and because of this symbiosis, you will feel driven, motivated, and inspired—all of which shall help you achieve success faster.

However, and this is very important, many of us do not know our talents. In fact, many of us go through life without ever knowing what we truly excel at. Do not get me wrong. Many of us are good at many things, but because of the popular doctrine that "talent is the one thing you should be great at," many of us go through life without ever discovering "our one thing." We move from one thing to the other looking for that "magical fulfillment" that comes from knowing and tapping into our talent.

Well, here is the thing, an irrefutable fact: *Talent is not all we make it out to be.*

Before you "string me up," consider the following.

Assume that as a child, you loved and excelled at football. You were the quarterback, a role you enjoyed and excelled at because you were naturally agile. Now, I want you to pay very special attention here. As you grew older, your priorities shifted and you stopped practicing or feeling intimately passionate about the sport. Does that mean that even if you do not practice, you will become a football legend? NO, it does not.

If you are naturally agile but fail to utilize the agility—which you do by engaging in activities that polish your agility—you will lose the agility. In fact, that is the case with most talents: when you don't use them, they fade into the background.

What does this tell you? It should tell you that *talent does not always translate into success.*

Having the potential and actualizing that potential are two different things. To achieve success, you need to do the latter: *actualize your potential.* This is why the advice given by most self-help books is great but only to some extent: because potential—and therefore success—in whatever field or career is something you can develop with deliberate and consistent practice.

When you know your strengths, you can capitalize on them and excel.

However, what about those of us who do not know our talents, does that mean we should be content with living mediocre lives? Does it mean we should be content with moving from this thing to the other, all the while hoping that one day we shall stumble upon our "natural calling?" NO. That is not the right way to approach the achievement of success.

When your talent hides like a shy moon on a cloudy night, it does not mean you shall never achieve success. It simply means you need to be practical about how you achieve that success.

In this guide, we shall be looking at success from a very different perspective. We shall be looking at how anyone, talented or not, can achieve great success in whichever area of life by taking very practical steps.

This guide tethers on one basic principle: **success is practice.**

Let me not sugar coat it for you—I know you are strong and can take a truth punch. If you want to become a great runner, you can become one even if running is not your "God-given" talent. If you want to become a great investor, you can even if numbers are not your strong suit. If you want to become anything or achieve anything, you can as long as you are willing to do one thing: **practice consistently**.

Consistent practice, what will Durant calls repeated habits, is what you need to achieve success.

Do not presume that this guide shall talk about doing something you hate just because you want to excel at it. Success should be enjoyable; so should the journey to achieving it. What this guide shall do is show you how to find exciting aspects of what you would like to do and achieve—even if you are not talented in it—and then consistently practice these elements so that in the end, you achieve great success and mastery.

Thanks again for buying this book. I hope you enjoy it!

Table of Contents

The first thing we shall do is dedicate a portion of the guide to discussing why consistent hard work trumps talent.

Success with No Talent: Why Talent Is Not All We Make It Out To Be

Look back at the story of Mo Farah. While he has the "talent," to achieve the success he has achieved as an athlete, he has had to practice consistently. If you examine the lives of many great people, people who have achieved success and recognition in their fiefdoms, you will note a replication of the same pattern.

In fact, I will reveal something to you:

What we call talent is actually manifested hard work. What we call talent is mastery over a specific domain. For instance, we can say that Warren Buffet is a talented investor or that Jeff Bezos is a talented manager. In actuality, what we mean is that these individuals have mastered something and are now great at it.

Business success boils down to this: *mastery over specific areas.* Buffet and Bezos have mastered their relevant domains, which is why we say they are talented. We can say the same of any other person: authors, athletes, life coaches, presidents, astronauts, etc. Those we consider "talented" are actually people who have practiced something so much that in the end, they have mastered it.

To achieve success, you need to do the same: master something. Mastery does not require talent. All it requires is **deliberate and consistent practice.** Take this to heart and make it your mantra. You can do, be, and achieve anything you are willing to sacrifice for—in this case, the sacrifice you have to make is put in the time.

Consider the following quote by Michael Jordan:

"I've missed more than 9,000 shots in my career. I have lost almost 300 games. 26 times, I have been trusted to take the game winning shot and missed. I have failed over and over and over again in my life. And that is why I succeed."

This quote is one of the most impactful you will ever read. It clearly illustrates that while being good at something (talent) is great, if you are willing to try as many times as it takes, you will be successful at anything.

Still in relation to Michael Jordan, consider this:

Throughout his long and successful career, Michael has scored 32,292 points, earned six NBA championships, and five NBA MVP titles. He has one of the most illustrious basketball careers in the record and many consider him one of the most talented and successful basketball players ever.

Did you know that as a 155.448-centimeter sophomore, Michael did not have a dunk to his name?

In 1978, Michael was an ordinary teenager who, like 50 or so of his schoolmates, was trying out for Emsley A. Laney High School Basketball team. The team had 15 roster spots and because he was short (5'10") he did not get one of the spots.

At that point, even though Michael was good at basketball—what we would call talented—the rejection could have devastated him because to anyone, it would have been an indication of lacking talent. Michael says that not making the team was embarrassing and after he went home, he locked himself in his room and cried to a point where he would have felt compelled to give up on basketball.

However—and this is something I want you to take keen note of and to heart—because he had the drive, he wanted to excel at basketball because he had CHOSEN it as his career path, he turned the pain of not making the team into motivation. He says:

"Whenever I was working out and got tired and figured I ought to stop, I'd close my eyes and see that list in the locker room without my name on it. That usually got me going again."

Consider this scenario very keenly. Jordan was a talented basketball player. However, that did not guarantee him a place on the team (even though his close friend, Leroy Smith who was 6'7" did). If when that happened, he would have decided, "I failed to make the cut because I'm not talented enough," would he be the person he is today? The answer is NO!

Talent has its limits. As is the case with Jordan, it can only take you a certain distance.

Because we live in a world where everywhere we look, we can see someone proclaiming that pursuing your talent is the best way to live a great and successful life, it is easy to allow ourselves to believe that success, or lack thereof, is talent based and that without talent, we shall amount to nothing.

Given, some people have a natural affinity to something: *they have a specific skill set that equips them for success in specific areas or careers.* Consider the example of someone who is naturally patient and a great listener. Because of this ability, such a person would excel in a field such as psychiatry or any other field that requires active listening. However, even in such an instance, there is no guarantee that the person would be a great fit for such a career because most times, success requires more than mere talent.

To succeed at something, you need to master and excel at it. Excellence, as Will Durant so rightfully puts it, *is habitual: the things you do every day.* In the case of Michael Jordan, after failing to make the team, he dedicated a large portion of his daily time to practice. It paid off handsomely.

Likewise, to achieve true success, you do not need talent. Yes, having a natural affinity for whatever you are pursuing is great, but it is not a prerequisite for success. Success requires but one thing: an **unwavering dedication to your cause.**

The following example should illustrate this:

Running is the simplest and most natural form of exercise. Our ancestors did it as they hunted, ran away from prey, and as they moved from one area to the other. As such, running comes naturally to us. Anyone can run. In fact, once a child learns to walk, running becomes the next, most logical step.

Running is also one of the best ways to remain physically and mentally healthy and is one of the greatest ways to lose weight.

Now think about this. If you had to guess—even a wild guess shall suffice—what would you say differentiates Mo Farah from the many runners who use the Nike App to guide their runs or the many others who run around the block or on treadmills?

The difference is not that Mo Farah is more talented, no. Whichever way you look at it, running is still running. The difference between Farah and other runners—if your go-to exercise is running around the block, you are a runner—is that he is more dedicated to it. He is so dedicated to it that he apportions a segment of his daily time to it. He is so dedicated to it that he has done all he can to master running, enhance his speed, and increase his endurance. What does this tell you? It should tell you that **dedication, not talent, is the prerequisite for success.**

If you examine your life closely, you will note that the accomplishments you are most proud of bred with an unwavering determination to achieve whatever you wanted to achieve at that point. On the other hand, if you examine your failures, you will also note that where you failed, you probably failed because you lacked the innate determination and dedication to succeed in that area of your life.

If life and success were a ladder, talent would be step 1. Step 2-10 revolve around determination and hard work. Does this mean talent is not important? No.

Some Words about Talent and Its Importance

It would be asinine for us to conclude that talent does not exist; it does. As indicated earlier, some people have a natural knack for specific things. However, and this is something I have found to be true across the board since the human DNA is very similar and only has slight variants—the variants that make your unique self—in essence, you can master anything anyone else has mastered. Yes, it may take time, but still, you can learn anything you consistently dedicate yourself to.

Take piano for example. Mozart was a talented piano player. Now, many ordinary piano players who have studied his music and playing style have become equally great piano players. It may have taken them longer than it took Mozart, but the fact remains that by dedicating themselves to the piano, ordinary piano players can turn into extraordinarily talented pianists.

Talent is great to have but excelling at something, even something you have a natural affinity for—a talent—requires dedicated hard work. Essentially, this means even if you lack the natural affinity for something, if you dedicate yourself to it, you will be good at it.

Because of our many prejudices about what it takes to get to the zenith of a specific field, to achieve success within a specific dominion, many of us opine that success comes to those who have natural gifts. You can see this manifest in how we talk about "he or she is so talented or lucky to be at the top of a specific area."

Success in life is like an iceberg:

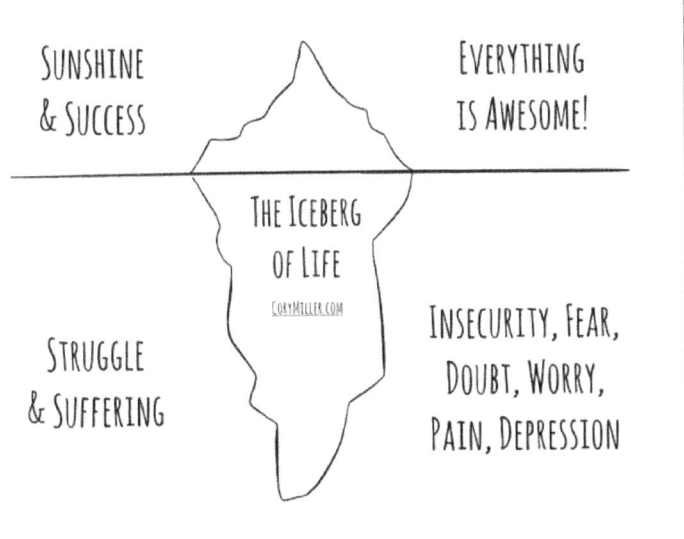

SUNSHINE & SUCCESS

EVERYTHING IS AWESOME!

THE ICEBERG OF LIFE

CopyMiller.com

STRUGGLE & SUFFERING

INSECURITY, FEAR, DOUBT, WORRY, PAIN, DEPRESSION

Image courtesy of copymiller.com

Outwardly, when someone is at the top of his or her field, what most people see is how great life is for that specific person. What they do not see is what lies underneath the iceberg: The hard work, the struggle, the fears one had to overcome, the pain of constant failure, the determination to overcome those failures and fears, the dedication to a certain cause, and the many other things it takes to achieve success.

To get to the top, you have to work hard; talent or being good at something is but a bonus. Here is what this guide shall unequivocally tell you: ***to achieve success, simply*** *find something you enjoy doing. You do not necessarily have to be good at it: just enjoy doing it*—enjoying something is not a prerequisite for success—it simply helps and makes pushing through that much easier.

If you have an interest in something, you will be willing to put in the work you need to put in to achieve the success you desire and deserve. Given, while some people have an affinity for something—they seem designed to fit specific roles or fulfill specific purposes—*talent is something you can build and grow through dedication and hard work.* Let that sink in. *Through dedicated hard work, you can develop any talent.*

Here is why many of us do not achieve success in life and business: we have *the wrong mindset.*

If you strongly believe that talent and success are one thing, you will never achieve success because you have the wrong perspective. When you believe that talent is what it takes to achieve success, you will build a negative mindset that will keep you from achieving success (because you believe you are not deserving of success because you are not talented).

When you think to yourself, "because I'm not good with numbers, I can never be as great at investing as Warren Buffet," you are shortchanging yourself because such a thought presupposes that to achieve success, you have to be just right: born under the right circumstances, experienced just the right things, developed just the right abilities, etc. As you can see, it is impossible to be "just the right fit" for a specific career or business.

When such thinking becomes your default-thinking mode, you are placing barriers on your path to success, a self-made wall that keeps you confined to your comfort zone. While talent is real—and indeed, this book acknowledges the existence of natural affinities—and makes a true difference in life, having or lacking talent is not an indicator of the success or lack thereof. In fact, lacking talent does not mean you cannot achieve success. Think of it this way; it is possible—an, in fact, doable: many people have done it—to be exceptionally great at something you lack the talent for and be talented at something but still lack success.

A Change of Perspective Is a Necessity

This guide asks you to do one thing: *change how you viewability.*

Your perspective, in this case, believing that "talent" is what it takes to achieve success, can keep you from doing many things. As we described earlier, holding on to this perspective shall cause you to build an impenetrable barrier that will keep you from achieving success and riches. When you think, "Because I am not naturally creative, I'll never be a great inventor," you are forcing upon yourself a self-made disability that will keep you tethered to failure and mediocrity.

This guide implores you—as a matter of importance—to stop looking at ability as natural talent. In fact, this guide explicitly asks you to stop labeling anything you are good at as talent. Instead, consider everything an ability. Those you

9

consider talented appear talented because they have mastered an ability.

What do we know about abilities? We know that abilities are learned behaviors. Those you consider talented appear so because they have mastered specific skills relevant to their specific areas. Take the example of Mo Farah. While he may be naturally talented, talent has very little to do with his success. He is successful because he has mastered the skill of running by adopting specific training strategies. The same applies to Jordan (and any other successful person you can imagine): they are successful because they have mastered a specific skill.

The change of mindset I want you to adopt right now—and make as natural a part of you as breathing—is that other peoples' seemingly innate abilities (talents) are mastered skills. From this day henceforth, when you see someone who appears naturally good at something, ask yourself, "which skills have this person mastered to become the person he or she is right now, to achieve the success he or she has achieved in his or her life?" If you do this, I guarantee you that you shall never look at "talent" the same way again. To you, everything shall start boiling down to, "which skills can I master to replicate the success X or Y person has achieved in his or her life or area of expertise?"

For instance, if you want to become the greatest investor the world has ever seen, you can ask yourself, "Which skills have great investors such as Warren Buffet, Benjamin Graham, Carl Icahn, and the likes had to master to become the persons they are and how can I make those skills part of my person?"

Can you see how this shift changes the dynamics of success? It changes everything because when you adopt this positive perspective towards success, success stops being about how naturally good you are at something and becomes more about which skills you need to master to achieve replicate success in your life.

When you start seeing talents as skills, you task your subconscious mind, the most powerful bio-computer the world has ever seen, a computer whose purpose in life is to give you answers to the questions you ask in the exact way you ask them, with looking for the underlying skills you can learn to replicate success in your life.

Tony Robbins, one of the world's greatest motivational speakers, says, *"Success leaves clues."* That is true; success does indeed leave clues, which is why one of the most powerful success strategies is to model successful people: do what they do, learn what they do, become them—without replicating everything: observe them and then make their strategies yours—and undoubtedly, you shall achieve similar or even better success because *Success leaves clues.*

I'm going, to be honest with you:

Yes, talent is real and it can accelerate success (because as we have said many times over, when you are good at something, you can strike a healthy balance between work and play).

However, and please, memorize this, take it to heart, and live your life by it, **success boils down to three things: passion—a strong liking for something—dedication—a burning want for something—and mastery of a skill—learned talent.**

These are words to live by. Words that when made yours and brought to life by your desire to achieve whatever you want to achieve, shall help you stop gawking at "talent" and instead of considering someone as "gifted," help you start looking underneath the hood to unearth the skills the specific person you want to emulate has had to master to achieve success.

Let's take this discussion further.

When Talent Does Not Work Hard, Hard Work Trumps Talent

We have talked much about how some people seem naturally gifted and able to do specific things well. We have also talked much about how, to excel, to achieve success at something you are "not naturally good at," you should change your mentality and instead of considering someone as naturally good at something, start looking at the underlying skills whose mastery has brought on the illusion of talent.

From the discussion in the previous section, you may be feeling super inspired and motivated because you are now aware that talent is just another word for mastered skills.

We shall continue the discussion we started in the last section but this time, we shall look at why talent is not "all that" and why it is possible to "appear talented" but still not achieve success.

The Nature of Our World

We live in a world where everything about our lives—from school, work, and even life outside work—seems to say you should be playing to your strengths, and capitalizing on your talent.

As this guide stated in the last section, even though our modern is all for equality, we cannot overlook the fact that some people are naturally great at some things.

NOTE: Some researchers have discovered that in our search for equality for all, we have overlooked the very fact that we are unique and therefore have unique strengths. In fact, a research study by Elizabeth Meinz and David Hambrick, a study that sought to determine the importance of talent, has discovered that domain-specific experience and knowledge greatly influence performance.

Take note of something here: *the words used.* In their bid to determine the importance of talent, Elizabeth and David use the words **domain-specific experience and knowledge**; this should only serve to tell you one thing: that even from a scientific standpoint, talents is actually domain-specific knowledge and experience, which loosely translated, means mastered skills.

In a paper published in 1993 by Ericsson, Krampe, and Tech-Romer, the trio stated that success is a fruit of deliberate practice in and usually:

"Builds upon purposeful, thoughtful, and intense efforts to improve performance over about 10,000 hours."

Although many researchers have contested the 10,000 hours rule—that to become great at something, you need to put in at least 10,000 hours of practice—many researchers agree that mastery over any dominion of life and business requires a lot of hard work and consist practice.

Think of it this way. Before Ma Yun, professionally called Jack Ma, the founder of and majority shareholder in Alibaba Group, could achieve the success he now enjoys, he had to lay the foundation for Alibaba, the business that later paid him handsomely and made him one of the richest men in the world. We can say the same for Warren Buffett and any other business leader you can think of: they got to where they are because they laid the foundation by putting in the hours or hard work.

When talking about this, I like to point out the story of The Beatles. The Beatles are one of the best bands to have ever existed. Do you know how they became so good, so good to a point where to the casual person, it would appear as if they were first in line when the universe or God was handing out musical talent? Well, they became so good because when they were living In Hamburg, they would dedicate a minimum of 4 hours a day 7 days a week to their music. We can say the same of many other successful people we would all want to emulate.

However, it's important that we ask ourselves if hard work trumps talent or makes it redundant. Does it mean that if you practice something for 10,000 hours, you will automatically excel at it all things considered?

The truth is that there is a correlation between talent and hard work. If you have a "talent," something you seem to be naturally good at, but fail to put in the work needed to polish it, you will not excel at it. On the other hand, if you have an interest in something, even something you are not naturally good at but is willing to practice it, to put in the work, you will be laying the foundation for success in the future.

Essentially, this spells out one thing: even if you lack "talent," even if "genius" in a specific field is not in your genes, with consistent practice, you can outshine people who others would consider naturally talented at specific things if all the "seemingly naturally talented" want to do is coast through life. This should tell you that while talent does indeed matter, mastery of a skill is more important. Mastering a skill takes a lot of deliberate and consistent work. □

If you are willing to put in the hard work, I guarantee you that you can master anything: anything. You can achieve success in whatever you set your eyes on. Yes, it may take you longer, and yes, while you may not be the best, you can be good enough to give a performance that rewards you handsomely in business.

I like to give this example.

Some people, at no fault of theirs, seem naturally good at starting and maintaining conversations. Perhaps because of upbringing, some seem to struggle with starting conversations and maintaining them.

This example is a great one in that even though some people appear born naturally good at starting conversations, for the most part, with consistent practice and clarity of thought, which in this case is to become better at the art of conversation, and being determined, even those who struggle with starting and keeping a conversation can master success in that area.

Yes, while inside of you is a natural affinity to something, achieving success in life and business will require more than affinity; even if you have no talent, you can achieve success because, at the end of the day, success is mastery over something. If you are willing to learn specific skills related to what you want to achieve, with hard work, determination, and continual improvement, you can become good enough to achieve success in any field of choice.

Being of modest talent does not mean you shall never achieve success. It simply means that to achieve success, you need to become practical about it. Determine the most basic skill you need to learn to achieve success in a specific area of your life and then commit to learning it and making continual progress every day. Eventually, as you gain mastery of the core skill—and every aspect of the business has a core skill whose mastery will make you good enough to achieve success—you will become someone who other people consider talented or lucky to have been born great at X or Y: success.

At this point in this guide, you already have all the knowledge you need to achieve success in any area of your choosing. Whichever area of business (or life) you seek to be successful in, if you stop saying you are not talented, if you drill down, consider the core skills you need to learn to achieve success in that area, if you then consistently practice those skills, you will achieve. No matter how long it takes, you will achieve mastery.

The remainder of this guide is going to take a practical approach to achieving success. The practical aspect of this guide will build on the tenet that to achieve success, you need to learn core skills in specific areas of your life. For instance, if you want to become a great athlete, consider the running strategies you need to learn, the healthy routine and diet you need to learn and adapt, and the consistency you have to practice as you put in the hard work to achieve mastery or running.

The same applies to business. If you want to achieve business success by being the greatest inventor the world has ever seen, to achieve success, you need to do things that enhance your creativity, and consistently dedicate time to enhancing your creative chops.

Building on this tenet, this guide is going to outline the 3 steps you need to implement to achieve success in anything, even things you don't seem naturally talented in. These three steps will ride on the shoulders of this basic principle: once you decide you want to achieve success in a specific area of life or business, even if you are not naturally good at that area, if you are willing to put in the work and do so consistently, you can gain mastery and its fruits, success!

The 2 things (actually, they are three but two overlap) we shall discuss will revolve around skills mastery, i.e. how you can go about mastering success in any area of life, even areas you don't feel naturally talented in or at. If you actually implement these three steps, you will achieve success; it's that simple!

Are you ready to learn the two things or steps you need to learn and master to achieve success in every area of your life, even areas where you don't seem naturally suited to? Let's discuss that next.

NOTE: This guide is not oblivious to aspects such as motivation and determination. Even though you can achieve success in any area, to achieve that success, you need to show a keen interest in being successful in that area because if you are not interested in what you want to achieve, you will not achieve it because your motivation and desire for it shall wane.

Master the Art of Goal Setting–The Most Important Step

If you only take one thing from this guide, let it be this: **_goal setting!_** If you become good at goal setting, I guarantee you that you will be a few steps closer to achieving whatever you want and will be in the top 10% of people who actually set goals.

This book has talked a lot about how, if you have clarity of vision and concentrated focus on your vision, you can achieve any success you want even in the absence of talent. In fact, this guide has gone to great lengths to show that talent is nothing more than mastery over a specific skill.

Think of it this way. I like Jeff Bezos, you want to create business wealth by tapping into online commerce, to achieve success, you need to examine Bezos's life. You need to determine the core skills he has had to learn and master, and then embark on making those skills part of your everyday personality until you can master them or become good enough to replicate his success.

Success boils down to that: **_learning the core skills that act as the foundation for the success you want to achieve._**

For instance, if you want to become a professional long distance runner, the core skills you need to learn and master are endurance and speed; endurance so that you can run longer and speed so you can run faster. Mastering these core skills will require that you learn other additional things. As an example, to improve your endurance and speed, you will have to adapt and master the correct running style, adopt a diet and strength training routine that is innately suited to what you want to achieve, and perhaps, in this case, learn how to rest and relax the muscles.

The same applies to business success. To achieve it, you need to learn core skills.

Before we start outlining the first step that is going to usher you into a new era of talent-free success in any area of your life, it is important to reiterate that talent is actually harnessed interest. Earlier, we talked about how talent can be fleeting when left unused. That is true.

If you closely observe the lives of successful people who have mastered a specific area and achieved success in that area, you will note that fundamentally, the area they now seem talented in morphed from an interest. Take the example of Warren Buffet.

From his biography, we know that he developed a keen interest in money and investing at a very young age (perhaps because his dad was a stockbroker-turned-Congressman or perhaps because he had a natural aptitude for money and business).

Buffet took such a keen interest in business and investing that at the age of 6, he used his savings to start his first business: buying packs of Coca-Cola for 25 cents each and reselling them for a nickel. Later on, at the age of 11, he made his first foray into the world of high finance by purchasing a share of Cities Service then offered at $38 per share.

Buffet is very popular for playing the long investing game, i.e. buying equity in a firm—buying shares—and then holding on to them until he feels ready to sell. He says he the Cities Services shares taught him that lesson because after holding onto the share until the stock price rose to $40, he sold them. Shortly after, Cities Service stock price rose to $200.

Yes, some say that from a young age, Buffet had a natural aptitude for numbers and could mentally calculate rows of numbers in a jiffy. Yes, his uncanny ability to invest may have come as talent, but here is the thing though. Buffet became so good at investing not because he was born a natural investor, NO! He became so good at it because he took a keen interest in it. He learned math (which is why he could seem naturally talented at calculating rows of numbers off the top of his head) and because he had clarity of vision, could cultivate the patience he needed to start saving and buying and holding shares until selling them was profitable for him.

You can read more about Buffet from the following book:

https://www.amazon.com/Snowball-Warren-Buffett-Business-Life/dp/0553384619

To achieve success, that is what you need to do: **become intimately interested in something.**

Achieving business success does not need you to be talented in your area of interest. Yes, having a natural aptitude for something is great, but it is not a prerequisite. All you need is a keen interest in whatever you want to achieve. If you have that, you can achieve anything you want; any level of success you can imagine can be yours.

Here is an example. Assume that you want to become the most sought-after financial consultant on Wall Street. However, you are not "naturally good" at reading charts or math.

NOTE: Remember what we said earlier: do not consider it a talent; consider it a skill, something you can learn.

To achieve success in this area and become the most sought-after financial consultant—to become so good at it that you appear naturally talented, as if you were born for it—you need to become better at reading charts and math, which is something you can do if you dedicate time to it every single day. It may not take you 10000 hours, but you will have to put in the time and work.

To feel motivated enough to develop such skills, you need to develop a keen interest in developing them because if you are not, you will not feel driven or motivated to pursue performance and then mastery. That is the core element of achievement: ***it requires that you develop a keen interest in what you want to excel at.***

Excellence is a very practical process that follows a path. Goal setting is the first step on this path.

Goal setting is a simple concept: choose what you want to achieve. This is very simple and straightforward. When you decide you want to achieve something, it means you have a keen interest in that thing.

First, goal setting reveals the things you have a keen interest in. Then, it walks you through the process of whittling down your interest to its bare minimum so that at the end of the process, you have a list of daily activities, practices, or things you can do to enhance your ability in that interest. Because success is habitual, when you do something daily for long enough, you develop a natural aptitude for it and at that point, interest starts becoming something deeper: innate motivation for something, which if we are being honest, is the very way we would define talents: a strong desire to do something.

About Goal Setting and Why It Matters so Much

Goal setting is an important part of the achievement process because, in the end, you become what you repeatedly concentrate on and do. If you concentrate on how talented you are not, you will feel defeated long before you start. On the other hand, if you concentrate on how you can improve a specific area of your life and business and then consistently dedicate time to this area of your life, you will get better through performance until eventually, you master that area.

Take an instance where you want to become a great salesperson so that in the next 3 years, you can run a marketing department—or your own marketing firm—but are not great at starting conversations with strangers or turning these contacts into buying customers.

In such an instance, if you concentrate on all the reasons why you cannot become a great salesperson, why you lack the natural aptitude for gab, you will lack the motivation needed to master the art of selling. On the other hand, if you show a keen interest in it and then turn this interest into daily consistent action, eventually, you will become a great conversation starter and shall be able to convert contacts into paying clients with ease.

That is what goal setting does: it helps you clarify what you want to achieve (what you are truly interested in) so that in the end, you feel motivated to put in the consistent hard work that will help you gain mastery of that field—not to mention success. Goal setting is so important a step that other than helping you achieve success in the area you want, it molds you into the person you need to become to achieve that goal.

For instance, if you want to become a great athlete, by dedicating time to goal setting, you can learn of all the things you need to do to become one and how much daily time you need to dedicate to the mastery of your sport of choice. When you do what you set out to do every day, the result will be a stronger spirit, better focus, and as you consistently put in the work, you shall mold yourself into the person you need to become to shape, achieve, and far outmatch your dreams.

Engaging in goal setting ensures that your focus on what you want to achieve, your area of interest does not wane or waver so that in the end, you can hone in on the exact skills and actions you need to take daily to achieve success in everything you choose to dedicate time and effort to.

This guide is going to outline very basically, but extremely powerful goal-setting strategies that when implemented, will give you clarity of thought and action so that in the end, whatever success you can imagine yourself having, you can manifest in your real life.

The nature of life is that we look long-term but live short-term. What does this mean? It means that although many of us dream of better futures, we live in the present, a present that can present many obstacles and temptations such as procrastination: the killer of dreams.

Goal setting allows us to clarify our vision for our lives so that in the end, because we have clarity of mind and action, we can look past the short-term obstacles that will undoubtedly manifest as we work towards achieving our long-term vision and success. When you set powerful goals, goals that interest and motivate you—meaning the goals you set out to achieve have to interest to you, ones you truly want to achieve—the daily motivation to act as you seek to master specific skills will appear to come naturally and therefore, you shall have guaranteed success no matter how long it takes.

How do you go about setting goals? Which key aspects of goal setting should you learn and remember as you write down your vision and set out to achieve it? Here are the key steps to goal setting. Use these steps to define, with clarity, how to achieve anything you have shown a keen interest in:

Step 1: Evaluation and Reflection

Talent is an amazing thing; amazing in that when you "have talent," you feel attracted and drawn to career paths that seem to play to your strengths. In instances where you do not feel naturally talented at something, goal setting is the ultimate strategy that will help you segregate what you want from what you do not want.

To manifest the successful future you desire, you need to know how you will get to that future. Think of success as a journey. Before you can start a journey, you need to pack and everything you will need for and while on the journey. You will need to take gradual steps to get to your travel destination. For instance, if you are traveling for a business conference, you will need to ensure your accommodation is right, your tickets are in order, you have the correct travel time and the likes.

Success is the same: to achieve it, you have to know where you are right now so that you can know what you need to do to get to the future success you want. The first step, therefore, is to give yourself time to reflect; to consider the kind of success you want to achieve, your current situation, and what it shall take you to achieve that success.

Evaluation has two purposes. The first is that it allows you an objective view of what you want to achieve, the vision you want to manifest in your life. Second is that it illuminates the present situation so that you can determine where you want to go and what you need to do to get there.

Dedicate a couple of hours of your day to evaluate and reflect. Write where your current state, your preferred future state—the success you want to achieve—and the several things you need to do—and skills you need to master—to make that future success a reality. This is very beneficial because when you have this in check, you will have a benchmark upon which to track progress. When you can track and see progress—no matter how minimal—the excitement of knowing that you are gradually achieving success shall inspire you to keep going.

Step 2: Define and Refine Your Aspirations

Achievement boils down to the clarity of thought and action. If you know what you want and how you intend to achieve what you want, you will achieve what you want: it is that simple!

Our desire for success is unquenchable: we all want better lives. When you closely examine our lives, you will note that goals are an integral part of it even when they do not appear clearly manifest or we fail to write them down. For instance, many of us want financial success, better lives for our families and our ourselves, better health, etc. Anything we do towards achieving this, whether that be being an employee or starting a business, working out or eating healthier, anything we do towards manifesting these desires in our present lives becomes a goal.

The amazing thing about us humans is that on top of having the innate desire to achieve, to have better lives, we also have the innate ability to plan how we intend to achieve whatever we want. That is what you need to do: whether you have or lack talent, to achieve anything, anything at all, you need to plan how you intend to achieve whatever you want to achieve.

At this point, give yourself the gift of time and at this time, do the following:

Consider what you want to achieve and then write it down. What are your aspirations or dreams and goals? What do you want to achieve? Give these questions proper thought because essentially, what you truly want does not build on what you have done thus far or what you already have.

Clearly define your values—your ideal life—and use it to define what you truly want. The thing about life is that many of us are living and pursuing lives we do not feel truly connected to or inspired to achieve. For instance, many of us want wealth—something that is OK to want—but very few of us actually take the time to define what wealth means to us: all we know is that we want more money, bigger houses, bigger cars, etc.

Take a moment to reflect and tune into your heart to learn what you truly want. This will help you develop a keen interest in the goals you are about to create. For instance, if after self-reflection, you discover that in your hearts of hearts, you want to start a business, you will develop a keen interest in entrepreneurship and in the process, reveal the important thing/skills you need to master to become a successful entrepreneur.

As you engage in this process, dig deep. Consider all the things that excite, thrill you, and get your heart pumping: these are your interests—you may or may not be naturally good at them. Regardless, you can achieve success in whatever field so long as you have the impassioned desire.

Consider this question; if your fairy godmother waved her magic wand and in an instant, you never had to work a day in your life ever again, what would you do for business, fun, or pleasure? What would you love to accomplish if, by a stroke of luck, you knew you could not fail? Whatever you come up with is the thing that interests you the most and what you should pay special attention to and pursue.

Write down what pops out, the dreams that fill your heart with excitement and joy. Go wild here. Untether your mind from the confines of "that goal or vision is too outlandish or foolish." If you can visualize it and then put in place a detailed action plan, you can achieve it.

Now that you have your most passionate goals, the things you want to achieve so badly that not achieving them pains you, the other thing you need to do is create a plan.

Step 3: The SMART Strategy

Now that your goals and aspirations are on paper, consider which of them are important and which ones are feasible. Which of these aspirations would you like to achieve most? Arrange all your aspirations in the order in which you would like to achieve them. The idea here is to arrange your aspirations from the most feasible ones, the ones that inspire you most, to the most outlandish ones so that instead of "just dreaming," you can actually get down to the nitty-gritty of taking action. The action is what brings success.

The SMART acronym is the best way to create goals, refine them, and then put in place an action plan that will help you manifest the achievements you want to see in your present life sometime in the future.

SMART means:

Specific

Measurable

Attainable

Realistic, and

Time-sensitive or *bound*

Specific goals have a clear definition. For instance, now that you know you want to go into entrepreneurship, what kind of business do you want to start? Do not be vague here. If you want to start an online, clearly define the type of online business you want to start. If you want to become a great athlete, clearly define the level of athleticism you want to achieve in your sport of choice.

Be very specific because if you are ambiguous, you will achieve ambiguous results and a future that does not match with your aspiration. This disconnect is why so many people that seem to have "made it in life" are so unhappy.

Measurable goals are goals whose progress towards you can measure. For instance, if your goal is to become one of the greatest distance runners in the 10K category, your goal is to complete the race in less than 26:17.53, which is the world record for that race. This goal is measurable because as you exercise, you can track how long you do a 10K run and use each run as a benchmark for future progress towards smashing Kenenisa Bekele's record.

Make sure the goals you create and choose to pursue are specifically measurable: they have an innate unit of measure so that you can know how you are progressing towards their achievement and most importantly when you achieve your goal.

Attainable goals are goals you can achieve. Yes, while you should "wild out" and create outlandish goals—if they are the ones that fill your heart with joy and drive it into a gallop—you should also make sure that you are pursuing goals you can actually achieve.

In the real sense, any goal is achievable but only if you are willing to make the sacrifice, which in this case does the work and do so consistently. Do not make the mistake of setting too outlandish goals. If you have a lofty goal, try to determine the most basic thing you need to achieve to drive yourself towards the final goal. This means you have to whittle down all your outlandish goals into smaller goals and then actively pursue these goals (preferably each day) until your final vision becomes a part of your daily life.

Realistic goals are real goal: goals you can, with reasonable effort and commitment, actualize in your life. Just as you should only pursue attainable goals, you should only pursue realistic goals. Ideally, even if a goal requires stretching outside your comfort zone and sacrificing somethings, as long as it's realistic, you can achieve it.

Take the example of an instance where you are currently earning $6000 per month but you want to increase it to $60000 in the next 2 months. Such a goal is unrealistic (unless of course, you have a well-laid out million dollar plan that has the potential to generate that kind of revenue in 2 or so months) because going from $6000 to $60000 in monthly earning is indeed unrealistic.

The idea here and the benchmark you should use to decide if a goal is realistic and attainable is to determine what you need to do to achieve it. For instance, if you would like to achieve this goal—the one of having a monthly income of $60000—which X, Y, and Z things do you need to do to achieve this goal? If you cannot whittle down a goal into the things you need to do to achieve it, that goal is unattainable and unrealistic.

Time-bound goals are goals that have an achievement deadline. You should always attach a deadline to all your individual goals. The pursuit of specific and individual goals should not go on indefinitely. All your goals must have a time frame: a date or time at which by, you will have accomplished that goal.

Attaching deadlines to your goal is very important because it allows you to see just how much work you have put in and how much more work you need to put in to achieve your set goals. This is very powerful because seeing how far you have come and how far you have to go inspires and motivates you to work diligently.

If you have an outlandish goal, break into down into its basic steps and process and then attach deadlines to these individual steps and processes. For instance, increasing your monthly earnings from $6000 to $60000 in 2 months is not a realistic goal. However, doing the same say, in the span of a year, is completely realistic. Saying, "I want to increase my monthly earnings to $60000 by the end of this year" is giving your goal a deadline.

Once you break down the goal into monthly, weekly, and even daily actions—the X, Y, & Z things you need to do to achieve that goal: the skills you must master and the person you must become—you can see your progress as yearend approaches.

If you follow this basic step and process, there is nothing on this earth—and even outside if—you cannot achieve. That is the power of goal setting: it gives you clarity of thought and action.

Before we move on to the other two things you need to do (remember that the two overlap), we have to mention that this basic step assumes that although you lack "talent or skills" in a specific area you want to excel in, you have a genuine interest in that area. Interest is very important because it's the foundation upon which your motivation breeds. Without interest, you shall lack motivation and without it—motivation—you shall fail to take action. Again, the action is what it takes to achieve success in whatever field.

With this basic step in check, the other things you need to do are take action, which requires discipline and to take this action consistently. Let's talk about these two things as compliments to what we have discussed in this section of the guide.

Discipline and Consistency: The Glue that Holds Everything Together

With your goals set, the only thing left to do is to start taking action.

Unfortunately, because we have long-term visions but live in the short-term, in the present moment, many of us sacrifice long-term vision for short-term gains. Scientifically, we call this procrastination. Procrastination is "the action of delaying or postponing something."

Essentially, procrastination, as it relates to the goals you have set and want to achieve, boils down to one thing: immediate gratification. If you want to start a business but whenever you have scheduled to do so, you consistently push the goal of creating a business plan to tomorrow and instead, watch another episode of your favorite TV show, you are procrastinating.

Not doing what you intended to do when you intended to do it—now that you have determined what you need to do every day to achieve the success you want in any area of your life and business—boils down to a lack of discipline.

Procrastination is the most common reason why many of us fail to achieve our goals. For this reason, instead of touching on how you can cultivate discipline, we shall discuss scientific strategies you can use to take consistent action— i.e. stop procrastination—and in the process, develop the discipline you need to stay the course until your goals and aspirations become your reality.

Master the art of pre-commitment

When you know you have no way out, you are likely to feel inspired to rise to the occasion. Pre-committing to a task or goal is one of the best ways to avoid procrastination and take action because it replicates the element of having no way out.

By pre-committing, we mean you should put your money where your mouth is. For instance, if, as you seek to increase your monthly earnings to $60000 per month, one of your micro quotas is to create a vibrant business plan, pre-commit a specific amount of money to the achievement of a goal within specified timelines. Every time you fail to achieve the said goal, you forfeit the money.

To add this element to your goal and keep yourself from procrastinating—and thereby chipping away at your discipline—I recommend using an app called stickK, an app that allows you to re-commit to your goals.

The great thing about pre-committing is that before you can actually set up a goal, you have to think about the X, Y, and Z things you need to do to achieve your goal, and after that, lay down some stake so that if you miss the deadline, you forfeit the stake. With stickK, the stake is money that the app donates to a charity you hate every time you fail to achieve a goal within a specific time.

You can also pre-commit to a goal by making a public commitment and sharing your plan with family and friend—or anyone who can keep you accountable. Accountability is a very lethal strategy against procrastination because when you know someone shall ask you to give an account of where you are in the process of achieving the goals you set out to achieve, the result is that you will not procrastinate.

Macro goal and Micro quotas

Our motivation to achieve specific aspirations comes from the goals we set and the plans we lay out for their achievement—, which is why this book implores you to, even if you lack talent, be intimately interested the area you want to achieve success in.

Procrastination and lack of discipline are, at the core, a lack of a strong enough reason to work on achieving the aspirations you have set out to achieve. Whenever you find yourself pushing forward things you ought to do today, perhaps you are doing so because you do not feel intimately interested in what you want to achieve?

Researchers investigating motivation have discovered that abstract thinking about goals can actually increase discipline. Dreaming big is great advice; however, to achieve success, you have to do more than just think big, you have to create a plan. If you find yourself procrastinating, pushing back the aspect of creating your plan, get started on creating macro goals and micro quotas.

Macro goals are the things you want to accomplish. On the other hand, micro quotas are the specific things you must do every day to achieve your macro goals. For instance, if your desire is to become a great business author, your macro goal could be to publish two books this year and your macro quota could be to write 2000 words every day of the week without fail. Micro quotas make outlandish goals approachable and achievable—it is the same thing as breaking down a big goal into smaller goals and milestones.

Quotas are important because they help you take it one moment, hour, day, or week at a time so that at the end, you take consistent action, gain discipline, and achieve your goals. They help you keep moving forward. As you set micro quotas, keep the bar low and build from there, and align them with your macro goal so that your motivation to achieve increases with each day you take action.

There you have it: the very things you need to do to achieve success even in areas you have no natural aptitude for. To complement the lessons you have learned in the last section of this guide, I recommend that you read the following guides on motivation, discipline, and taking consistent action.□

https://www.positivityblog.com/how-to-improve-your-consistency/

https://www.forbes.com/sites/jennifercohen/2014/06/18/5-proven-methods-for-gaining-self-discipline/#1c6b2e253c9f

http://happierhuman.com/now-not-later/

http://happierhuman.com/difficult-not-easy/

http://happierhuman.com/performance-or-mastery/

Conclusion

We have come to the end of the book. Thank you for reading and congratulations on reading until the end.

My greatest desire is to see you become successful. Implement the ideas and strategies we have discussed in this guide: they will help you achieve success in any area you choose even if you have no natural talent or lack the innate skills needed to thrive in that area

If you found the book valuable, can you recommend it to others? One way to do that is to post a review on Amazon.

Please leave a review for this book on Amazon!

Thank you and good luck!